THE

YORKS

C000078216

25 MILES FROM HORTON IN RIBBLESDALE
SCALING 3 OF THE HIGHEST PEAKS IN
YORKSHIRE ON A CIRCULAR ROUTE

AN ESSENTIAL GUIDE TO HELP YOU
COMPLETE
THE
YORKSHIRE 3 PEAKS WALK

BRIAN G SMAILES

The Author

Brian Smailes

Holds the record for the fastest 4 and 5 continuous crossings of the Lyke Wake Walk over the North York Moors. He completed the 210 miles over rough terrain on 5 crossings in June 1995 taking 85 hours and 50 minutes.

Brian lectures on outdoor pursuit courses and between these travels extensively on walking expeditions and projects around Great Britain.

Long distance running and canoeing are other sports he enjoys, completing 24 marathons and canoeing the Caledonian Canal 3 times.

Other books by the same author:-

You will never walk alone with these books
published by Challenge Publications

THE SCOTTISH COAST TO COAST WALK
ISBN 0-9526900-8-X

THE COMPLETE ISLE OF WIGHT COASTAL FOOTPATH
ISBN 0-9526900-6-3

THE YORKSHIRE DALES TOP TEN
ISBN 0-9526900-5-5

JOHN O'GROATS TO LANDS END
ISBN 0-9526900-4-7

THE LAKELAND TOP TEN
ISBN 0-9526900-3-9

THE NATIONAL 3 PEAKS WALK
ISBN 0-9526900-7-1

THE 1066 COUNTRY WALK
ISBN 1-903568-00-5

THE NOVICES GUIDE TO THE LYKE WAKE WALK
ISBN 09526900-1-2

THE DERBYSHIRE TOP TEN
ISBN 1-903568-03-X

MILLENNIUM CYCLE RIDES IN 1066 COUNTRY
ISBN 1-903568-04-8

ISBN 1-903568-01-3
First Published 2001
CHALLENGE PUBLICATIONS
7, EARLSMERE DRIVE, BARNSLEY. S71 5HH
www.chall-pub.fsnet.co.uk

ACKNOWLEDGEMENTS

In publishing this 2nd edition of The Yorkshire 3 Peaks Walk I must thank the following people for their help and contribution :-

Pam Smailes
Geoff Whittaker & Janet Crossley for Photographs
Graham Fish
Trevor Atkinson for Sketch Map

ISBN 1-903568-01-3

*Published by:- Challenge Publications,
7 Earlsmere Drive, Barnsley, S71 5HH
www.chall-pub.fsnet.co.uk*

Printed by:- Dearne Valley Printers Ltd. Tel: 01709 872188

CONTENTS

USEFUL INFORMATION

PHOTOGRAPHS

ILLUSTRATIONS

FOREWORD

May we bid you a welcome to the Yorkshire Dales
and this Three Peaks guide by Brian G Smailes
There is a lot of information for all to find
with the novice walker being kept in mind
Before you start your journey up Pen-y-ghent
just call at the café it is money well spent
The proprietor there will gladly give you a talk
on his clocking system for The Three Peaks Walk
It is a good system that I recommend you use
the service is free so you've nothing to lose
You just have to clock out when the walk you begin
and at the end of your journey you clock back in
The simple thing that you have to do next
it to follow the route that's in Brian's text
Having completed the walk you may like to make
an attempt on The North York Moors Lyke Wake
and finding the way shouldn't be hard for you
for Brian has wrote a guide on that too.

Geoff Whittaker

The Yorkshire 3 Peaks Walk presents a challenge to any walker, to scale three of the highest peaks in Yorkshire.

Situated in the Yorkshire Dales National Park, the 3 peaks of Pen-y-ghent, Whernside and Ingleborough nestle together around the village of Horton in Ribblesdale.

This 2nd edition of The Yorkshire 3 Peaks Walk is fully updated and now includes B&Bs and a pull out sketch map showing the full walking route. Read the following pages carefully then go and enjoy this exhilarating walk.

INTRODUCTION

Walkers travel from throughout Britain to climb the 3 peaks in this picturesque part of Yorkshire. The distance of 25 miles on this circular walk can be quite strenuous but with some training and the careful selection of equipment to protect you from the elements, most people can accomplish this walk.

It usually takes between 9-13 hours to complete this walk. Some people run the course while others prefer a leisurely walk, staying overnight in a local B&B or camping on route.

The Pen-y-ghent café/tourist information centre in Horton in Ribblesdale operates a unique safety system. When used correctly it should ensure that nobody is unaccounted for at nightfall and no walker is lost up in the mountains without anyone knowing, more details further on.

All bearings are given as magnetic, 5° added to grid compass bearing from the map. True north is estimated at 5° west of grid north in 1999 decreasing by ½° in 4 years.

The route has suffered from erosion in parts but careful preservation by staff and volunteers from various organisations have restored some areas to their former glory.

In the interests of the environment it is recommended that walkers are in small groups on this walk and only the defined paths are used to help prevent further erosion of this beautiful scenic area.

THE YORKSHIRE DALES

The Yorkshire Dales begins near Skipton in the south and is bordered by Settle, Ingleton and Sedberg to the west, Tan Hill to the north with Leyburn and Richmond to the east.

It is an area of natural beauty with mountains, limestone and gritstone fells, woodland and rivers.

There are numerous unspoilt villages throughout in typical Yorkshire style, displaying all the charm and elegance of a timeless age.

The area is a paradise for walkers and cyclists, where you can forget your car and enjoy the countryside. Those who prefer more active pastimes can visit the numerous potholes, caves and cliffs for climbing and exploring above and below ground.

The famous Settle-Carlisle railway crosses Ribblehead Viaduct (which you pass) on its journey. You may see train spotters there if a steam train is due, eager for a glimpse as it crosses the viaduct.

There are market days in most towns like Skipton (Mon. Wed. Fri. Sat.) Settle (Tues.) Hawes and Richmond (Sat.), offering local and national products to discerning visitors from around the world.

THE YORKSHIRE DALES
& THE 3 PEAKS

DURHAM

TAN HILL

RICHMOND

CUMBRIA

• HAWES

NORTH YORKSHIRE
DALES NATIONAL PARK

WHERNSIDE

INGLEBOROUGH   PEN-Y-GHENT

• HORTON IN RIBBLESDALE

LANCASHIRE   SETTLE   GRASSINGTON

SKIPTON

ACCESS TO THE YORKSHIRE DALES

By Road:- The M6 passes Howgill Fells to the west, exit at J36 then follow the A65 towards Settle. The A1 passes to the east of Richmond and the main A610 from there leads onto the A684 into the Dales. From the south the Dales can be reached from the M62, turning off to Bradford then Keighley and following the A629 to Skipton. Bus/coach driving time from Bradford to Skipton is approximately 1hour. National coaches provide services to the larger towns e.g. Skipton and Richmond, where you can then connect with local transport to take you to your intended destination. Check with a T.I.C. for current coach times.

By Rail:- There are local stations in Skipton, Horton in Ribblesdale, Dent, Settle and Ribblehead. The southern Dales area is covered by the Leeds-Skipton-Carlisle line which passes over Ribblehead Viaduct and you can exit at Horton in Ribblesdale for your 3 peaks walk. Visitors to the area are encouraged to travel by public transport or bicycle to help cut pollution and congestion in the dales. Timetables change so please contact either the National rail enquiries or T.I.C. for current times of trains.

By Air:- There are two main airports covering the area, Leeds-Bradford and Manchester.

Telephone numbers for T.I.Cs, coach, air and rail enquiries are given in the back of this book to help you to confidently plan your journey and walk.

THE GEOLOGY OF THE AREA

The Yorkshire Dales area is principally a limestone base dating from the carboniferous period although there is evidence below this of Ordovician and Silurian rock strata.

This limestone was formed when corals and sea creatures died, their shells thus creating this base. It took millions of years and numerous climatic changes to lay down this limestone layer. Further changes took place resulting in layers of sandstone, shale and mudstone being deposited through a glacial drift down the valleys.

To finish the geological strata of the area, a deposit of millstone grit was laid down in the tributaries of a river which flowed through the area on its journey to the sea. Some peaks have this deposit of millstone grit covering them, but the valleys gradually became covered with plants, trees and swamps, resulting in some coal deposits being found in the north of the area.

When rain, frost and sun weathers the limestone, it becomes scarred with cracks and fissures, worn from the rock above and below ground, resulting in the many pot holes in the area.

Around the Ingleborough plateau in particular you can see the fields of limestone outcrops with their fissures and gullies like spiders webs, entrapping the careless feet of any walker who ventures over it in a casual manner. Walking the 3 peaks will involve navigating between these limestone outcrops and over rock formations, so take care. I am sure you will find the geological structure of the area fascinating to see, as I still do after many visits.

PREPARATION

When preparing for this walk, you have to remember there is a lot of climbing up and down, therefore knees and ankles should be in good working order before you leave.

Although the distance is only 25 miles, any walker attempting this walk needs to be reasonably fit, so training the weeks before the walk is recommended. Start walking short distances two months before the event, then gradually increase your distance walked, ensuring you incorporate some hills into your training routes. Build up to 20 miles if possible during training over rock, grass and moorland terrain. This training should ensure you are reasonably fit to complete the 3 Peaks.

Other types of fitness training e.g. cycling, keep fit sessions, jogging and swimming will all increase your fitness and stamina and help to prepare you for this undulating course.

Training in the use of basic map and compass work would be helpful especially if the peaks are covered in cloud as often happens in bad weather.

Consuming high energy food before and during the walk is most beneficial. Food with a high level of carbohydrate such as rice, pasta, potato, banana, malt loaf and milk will help to build up your energy reserves before the walk. While walking, glucose based sweets, apples and Kendal mint cake will all help to supply your body with extra energy as will isotonic drinks.

Finally, from past experience, those who do some type of exercise and do not drink or smoke heavily, usually complete this walk. Those who do nothing and drive from A to B do not!

EQUIPMENT SELECTION

When considering equipment and clothing for this walk, you must remember that it may be a calm, still, and what seems like a nice day in Horton in Ribblesdale but nearing the summit of any mountain it can be cold and very windy with low cloud. Often it is the wind chill factor that causes problems for walkers. With this in mind, the following suggested list of items should help you to both complete the walk and stay warm, dry and hopefully injury free.

1. Compass and guide book
2. Walking boots/fell boots
3. Walking socks including a spare set
4. Walking trousers (no jeans)
5. Warm upper body clothing (in layers),
    Spare clothing
6. Gloves, Woollen/fleece hat
7. Torch with spare bulb and batteries
8. Whistle, Note paper and pencil
9. Toilet paper
10. Survival bag
11. Basic first aid kit including plasters and vaseline
12. Fleece/waterproof fabric outer jacket/cagoul,
    overtrousers
13. Day rucksack
14. Food, Plastic drinks bottle (small)
15. Camera
16. Map of the area O.S. Yorkshire Dales. No. 2

Use this as a checklist before you leave. In addition to the above items, a complete change of clothes should be available at the campsite/bed and breakfast or in your car at Horton in Ribblesdale ready for when you return.

THE BODY

RUCKSACK
*Containing food, drinks,
first aid, clothing,
map and compass.*

THE HEAD
*Should be kept warm,
more heat is lost
from the head
than anywhere else.*

THE BODY
*Should be kept
warm.
Build clothes up
in layers with
wind/waterproofs
on top.*

MAIN BODY CORE
*Temperature must
be maintained.*

HANDS
*Should be kept
warm
with gloves.*

LEGS
*It is important not to
wear jeans*

ANKLES
*Should be
protected
by wearing boots,
to help strengthen
them.*

FEET
*Should be kept well
cushioned and dry if possible.
Good fitting boots will help
prevent blisters*

HYPOTHERMIA

Hypothermia is caused when the body core temperature falls below 35°C. If a walker is not properly prepared for the conditions or the equipment/clothing is not satisfactory then a combination of the cold, wet, exhaustion and the wind chill factor can give a walker hypothermia.

Ways of Preventing Hypothermia

1   Build up body clothing in thin layers, adding on or taking off as necessary.
2. Have suitable wind/waterproofs with you.
3. Take some food/hot drink or boiled sweets which produce energy and heat during digestion.
4. Wear a balaclava/woolly hat to insulate the head, and some gloves.
5. Shelter out of the wind.
6. Take a survival bag and if conditions dictate, use it.

In any type of emergency/accident situation it is always advisable to come off the mountain as soon as possible especially in fog, snow or other bad conditions. The temperature difference between the valley and the summit can be several degrees. If the injured walker is able to move safely, going down the mountain is usually the best solution.

When conditions do not permit movement and if you are in a sheltered area, stay where you are until such time as conditions improve. It may be at this time that you put on extra clothing and use survival bags.

Treatment for Hypothermia

1. Provide extra clothing and shelter from the elements.
2. Bodily warmth of others helps in a gradual warming.
3. If well enough come down into a warmer sheltered area.
4. Give hot drinks if conscious.
5. Give chocolate or sweets if the patient can still take food.
6. The casualty should be placed so that the head is slightly lower than the body.

DO NOT *rub the skin or use a hot water bottle as this can cause a surge of blood from the central body core to the surface, this could prove fatal.*

Alcohol should not be consumed on any walk and should not be given to anyone who has hypothermia. The body temperature will be lowered as well as giving a false sense of security.

Plate 1

Ascending Pen-y-Ghent, the path and stile is left of centre

Plate 2
Walkers ascending Pen-y-Ghent.

SAFETY SYSTEM

Pen-y-ghent café operates a unique safety system; before you leave Horton in Ribblesdale you can register details of your intending walk or other activity at the café. There is a card to complete and the following details are required :-

Name	Tel. No.
Home Address	Time of Departure
Reg. No. of Vehicle	Where Parked

Local/Hol. Address if not Returning Home Tonight.
A multiple or 'early bird' booking out sheet is available, ask in café.

After completing the card there is a clock card machine to register your start time. Hand the card in at the counter before leaving. As soon as you return to Horton in Ribblesdale you should go back to the café and ask for your card to 'clock back in'. This is extremely important because if you do not call back in a reasonable time then you could be reported missing and a search initiated.

Following the above procedure is simple and there is no charge for this service. There are some exceptions to the above procedure as follows:-

If you leave before the café opens, you can put all the above details on a piece of paper and put through the letter box.

The safety service does not operate on Tuesdays or Fridays.

The café is normally open 9am-6pm Mon. Wed. Thurs. Fri. and 8am-6pm weekends (summer), but if any walker has not returned, the café will stay open until all walkers are accounted for. The latest time you can depart is 9.30am if you are using the safety service.

Pen-y-ghent café is fully networked with the English Tourist Board (tourist information centre) and can assist with accommodation, parking advice and general information

Should your return be delayed for any reason and you cannot 'clock back in', then you should telephone 01729 860333 (café) to avoid a search being initiated.

Those who use the safety system and complete the 3 Peaks Walk within a 12 hour period are eligible to join the 3 Peaks of Yorkshire Club and wear the exclusive badge and tie. Membership is by invitation only, and by complying with the safety rules. Use the system wisely and be assured that at least someone knows you are out in wild country and have not yet returned.

Plate 3
On route to Ribblehead

Plate 4
The short road section before Ribblehead.

SUPPORT TEAM

Some people attempt this 3 Peaks Walk using a support team who meet them at each of the two check points and provide walkers with food and drinks. Walkers should be aware of the distance and approximate walking times between checkpoints and decide whether they can walk to the next checkpoint or retire honourably at the one they are at.

A good support team will give verbal encouragement as well as hot food and drinks to the walkers. When arriving at a checkpoint, walkers should not have to wait for food and drinks. These should be ready when the walkers arrive. Too long spent at a checkpoint will result in walkers feeling stiff and tired. As the walk progresses, the time spent at a checkpoint becomes more critical as the body becomes stiffer.

The two checkpoints are Ribblehead Viaduct at G.R.766793 which is 5.8miles (9.3Km.) from Horton, and The Old Hill Inn at G.R.743777. Distance 1.8miles (2.9Km.) from Ribblehead.

A good safety precaution is for the support team to operate a check in system at each checkpoint where walkers report in to the driver on arrival. Taking this precaution should ensure no walker has gone astray between checkpoints.

All support teams should have a supply of first aid equipment as well as sleeping bags and torches, also an emergency rucksack with the necessary equipment to assist walkers in difficulty. The success or failure of individuals or the whole group depends in some situations on how good the support team are overall. A good support team should have a responsible leader who will have basic first aid skills and be a competent map reader.

THE ROUTE IN DETAIL

PEN-Y-GHENT

Turn right from the car park (charge) in Horton in Ribblesdale and proceed to the Pen-y-ghent café which is about 50 metres along the road on your right. After using the free safety service in the shop, turn right and continue along towards the church which you will see at the south end of the village. You will pass Holme Farm campsite on your right where you cross the road.

Just past the campsite there is a small field on your left with a narrow wooden gate, turn left here. The church is a short distance away now to your right. Proceed through the next two small gates ahead of you then turn left onto a metalled road. You will see a bridge over the stream about 35 metres further on. Cross over the wooden footbridge and turn left onto a metalled road, passing the local school.

Continue on the metalled road keeping the stream on your left until you come to a farm at Brackenbottom where there is a signpost pointing to 'Pen-y-ghent summit 1¾ miles' G.R. 817723. Turn left here through a five bar gate, go over a stile then turn left along by a stone wall. The grass path now starts to ascend steeply and there are many ruts in the path.

You arrive at some stone steps in the wall ahead of you and Pen-y-ghent appears directly ahead. Continue ascending over 2 sets of stone steps and over 2 large stone outcrops, generally keeping alongside the stone wall in the direction of Pen-y-ghent. This area is known

Plate 5
The Aquaduct and path to Whernside.

Plate 6

Ascending Whernside. Your path is on the right with Force Gill Waterfall on the left.

as Brackenbottom Scar. Looking behind you can see Ingleborough in the distance with Horton in the valley and the quarry behind. Nearing the base of Pen-y-ghent there are 2 sets of wooden steps side by side going over a wall. As you continue to ascend steeply you climb a flight of man made stone steps, laid to combat footpath erosion. You come to another 2 sets of wooden steps over a wall, you now have a view of the east side of Pen-y-ghent *(plate 1)*. This area is an important site for ground nesting birds.

The shale and stone path to the summit is steep and care should be taken, *(Plate 2)*. As you approach there are some steep steps up the large rock outcrop. The path starts to flatten out before the final short ascent to the summit and the triangulation pillar, 'trig' point number S5776. Enjoy the view in all directions, weather permitting.

Near the triangulation pillar are 2 sets of steps over the stone wall, go over and you should see your path going downhill bearing 350°M from the stile. Follow the path for 300m then it turns right, still descending. **N.B.** This path is reasonably obvious.

Halfway down the hill you will see another distinct path on your left, which looks white. This path leads back to Horton in Ribblesdale and is part of the Pennine Way. A pile of stones marks the turning. It is useful if you decide to climb only one mountain then return to Horton.

After passing this path on your left, continue on the main path bearing 316°M from the junction at G.R.838742. The path veers left for a short distance then appears to run parallel with the path that leads back to

Horton. The paths are approx. 200m apart. The worn grass path in the distance ahead takes you to Horton Moor, leading to Ribblehead in the distance.

Following the path you arrive at a wet and boggy section, after crossing this and a small brook beyond, there is a stone wall in front. Go over the stile and cross a stream (which may be dried out during summer). Go over 2 more stiles to a wider stream, known as Hull Pot Beck. This is a pleasant area for picnics.

After crossing the stream, you go over numerous undulating small hills and the main area of natural springs. All this area is usually very wet, even in summer, so navigate over it and the numerous ditches, gullies and dykes carefully for this 550m stretch. This area is known as Black Dub Moss.

You go through an opening in a stone wall then over some stone steps crossing another wall *(plate 3)*. Proceed over the small hills still walking in the general direction of Ribblehead Viaduct. It is undulating for another mile, with good views all around as you cross the Pennine Way. Go alongside the stone wall in front of you, then bear left across a grass field keeping the limestone rock pavement on your left. Walk through another opening in a stone wall. The path turns to gravel and grass before crossing a narrow road which leads to a farm on your right. There are some fir trees on your left, with Dismal Hill 388m to your right at G.R.804770.

After crossing this road go down a narrow path still heading towards Ribblehead. Cross a stile and follow a rutted farmers track. You are now walking on part of The Ribble Way. You see a stone wall on your left and as the path bends round to the left, bear right across the grass by the side of the wall. Cross a stile at the side of a gate,

Plate 7
The steep descent from Whernside.

Plate 8
A winter ascent of Ingleborough with the path from Humphrey Bottom in bottom left corner.

following the undulating path, which is good in parts then it becomes just a farm track.

Turn left over a stile approaching a farm, then cross a small field before turning right through the farmyard at G.R.793778. Go over the next stile beside the farmhouse, known as Nether Lodge, onto a good flat farm road for 800m following the signpost pointing to Ribblehead.

Cross a cattle grid then pass over a bridge which spans the upper reaches of the River Ribble. You soon start to ascend on a winding path to pass Lodge Hall. As you pass the farm there is a tarmac road and on your left a spring with some good refreshing drinking water. Follow this narrow road up to the main B6479 road. Cross the cattle grid there then turn right *(plate 4),* walking for 1 mile (1.6km) to the junction at Ribblehead Viaduct at G.R.766793. At the junction there is a sign pointing to Ingleton to your left. You walk straight across heading towards the far end of the viaduct, which has 24 arches.

WHERNSIDE

At the junction there is a stream and often a refreshment van and is a popular picnic spot, G.R.766793. Carry on towards the viaduct keeping to the right of it and following the path to the far end before turning right up a small hill with a stone wall on your left at G.R.759797. The Settle/Carlisle railway is parallel with your path as you now walk to Blea Moor signal box.

Your path turns to shale chippings as you proceed around the northerly side of Whernside. You come to a stile, go over and continue on this undulating path for 800m to pass Blea Moor signal box and the recently renovated old railway house. This next section takes you over 2 small brooks (which may be dry) and the path is very stony and uneven. You cross a wide stream that is littered with stones but easily passable. This area is known as Blue Clay Ridge.

Nearing a stone wall continue on the path, which goes between 2 stone walls and cross the railway bridge. Walk around the picturesque aqueduct *(plate 5)* at G.R.761816, go over a stile and start to ascend. You will see the path which you need to take ahead of you. A signpost nearby states 'V.W. Dentdale 4 miles' in your direction of travel.

On your left you should see Force Gill waterfall, *(Plate 6)*. Go over a stile, you start to walk anticlockwise up Whernside. About halfway up there is a stile going over a wire fence. You are now ascending towards the summit on an obvious path. The area around here can be boggy so stay on the stone slabbed path and your feet should remain dry. The slabbed path takes you directly to the summit of Whernside. On approaching the summit, Pen-y-ghent can be seen off to your left and Ingleborough straight ahead.

Below Whernside there is Greensett Tarn, which looks inviting on a hot day. On the summit on a clear day you can see Morecambe Bay to your right and the mountains of the Lake District to your extreme right.

Continue from the summit on a dusty small stone path on bearing 201°M from the main path beside the 'trig' point. The limestone plateau that surrounds Ingleborough can be clearly seen. You descend 2 short steep slopes which are stony and uneven. Follow the stone wall down for 1.2km then the path turns left away from the summit on bearing 162°M at G.R.735804, towards Bruntscar *(plate 7)*.

When taking this new path, extreme care should be taken as the route down is stony, uneven and can be dangerous for about 60m, one slip could send you rolling down the hill. Further down, the path becomes gravel and easier to walk on as you make the gradual descent to the valley and farms you pass on the way.

Cross 2 stiles, then just past the farm building turn left at G.R.739790. There is a metalled road, and in front, a small wooded area and ancient settlement at G.R.742784. This narrow road takes you past another farm building on Philpin Lane where there is a snack bar, and eventually to the main road. Turn left at the main road and a short distance ahead you come to the Old Hill Inn and the camp site at G.R.743777. This area is known as Chapel le Dale.

INGLEBOROUGH

When you leave The Old Hill Inn, there is a small stile just above it on your right, hidden by 2 trees. Go over and cross the field G.R.745776 then cross several stiles in the general direction of Ingleborough. The path is fairly obvious here. On your left side as you proceed you pass numerous limestone escarpments. The stone chipping path takes you through an area of limestone outcrops.

You pass a large pit or disused quarry on your left as you approach the base of Ingleborough. This is called Braithwaite Wife Hole, G.R.744763. Continue to a stone wall then over a stile onto a wooden boarded path which you walk on to the base of Ingleborough. This area is known as Humphrey Bottom G.R.746752.

At the base of the mountain you should see a path rising steeply up to the summit alongside a small stream. This zig zag path is very steep so extra care needs to be taken *(plate 8)* G.R.747749. Nearing the summit a signpost states 'National Nature Reserve' and 'Welcome to Ingleborough'.

Go through a swing gate and you have your last short steep climb to the summit. At the top of the steps, on your left, is the path you need to take you back to Horton in Ribblesdale G.R.745747, marked by a cairn. Continue up the steep rocky outcrop to 2 cairns on the summit, with a four way wind shelter in view directly ahead.

Ingleborough summit has a flat rocky plateau with a 'trig' point near the four way wind shelter. On the top of it is a plaque depicting the views in each direction.

In low cloud or if disorientated, a compass bearing of 80°M from the wind break should take you back to the 2 cairns. Retrace your steps now to the cairn which marks the path back to Horton (mentioned in the last paragraph). Turn right at the cairn on bearing 99°M and descend on a muddy and stony path over Simon Fell Breast. Horton is now in the valley ahead with Pen-y-ghent behind.

You now walk on a grass path and go over a stile. A sign pointing to Horton is just past it followed by a large limestone outcrop at G.R.774736. Your path runs between the limestone and undulating small hills. Continue in a straight line towards Horton passing another signpost stating 'Horton 1½ miles' (experience says it could be further).

Cross another stile onto a stony path where an opening through a stone wall leads to a large expanse of limestone rock. This area is known as Sulber Nick. The path turns to the right, pick it out carefully as you walk. The limestone rock diminishes and there are now fields, usually with animals in.

Cross the fields initially following the cairns on a narrow, undulating path with stiles over the stone walls. You will see a small tarn below the quarry. As you approach the railway line you see a sign 'Horton in Ribblesdale' at the small station. Cross the line with care and continue down the path and along the road in front towards the car park in the village.

There is a small bridge over the river on your right. Go over this and you are back in the car park. Return to the café and 'clock back in'. You are now free to partake of refreshment in a local hostelry and congratulate yourself on completing The Yorkshire 3 Peaks Walk!

ESCAPE ROUTES

When climbing any peak, accidents can happen or cloud can descend quickly causing problems for unwary walkers. You may find your intended route is hard to find or you are heading into bad weather. In this situation you have a choice, retrace your steps back to safe ground (you will need to know where you have been) or go forward using a compass if necessary. **N.B.** it is good practice to sight compass and map before entering fog or poor visibility. Alternatively you can use an escape route which is designed to give you the quickest route back to a safe area, though not necessarily back to your intended destination.

The following 3 escape routes can be used as the quickest route down from the summit of the 3 peaks.

Pen-y-ghent G.R. 839734

The shortest route from Pen-y-ghent summit to the nearest road at G.R.842714 is S.S.W. from the summit bearing 231°M on the Pennine Way then turning in a south easterly direction after 1800m on bearing 131°M for a further 1000m.

Whernside G.R. 738814

The shortest route from Whernside summit to the nearest road at G.R.722818 is in a westerly direction bearing 282°M from the summit. Follow a path for 900m descending, then walk for 150m on bearing 350°M. Now take a bearing of 282°M following a wall for 1150m down to the road.

Ingleborough G.R. 741746

The shortest route to a road at a lower level is to The Old Hill Inn at G.R.743776. From the summit bear 72°M for 700m going quickly downhill. After going through the gate, pick up a path going directly downhill bearing 9°M from the gate, off the peak towards Humphrey Bottom. Follow the path from the base in the same general direction back to The Old Hill Inn (extreme caution descending the zig zag path).

It is important to re-state that all bearings given in these emergency descent routes are magnetic bearings. Magnetic north is estimated at 5° west of grid north in 1999 decreasing by about ½° in four years.

Remember to inform Pen-y-ghent café if you cannot get back to Horton and you have used the safety system. Should you be able to reach a telephone then call 01729-860333 to inform them of your present position. In case of major problems dial 999 asking for cave rescue at Settle police station.

At night if you are lost but are warm and unhurt, try to go carefully on a path down to the lower slopes off the peaks and out of the wind. Put on warm clothing and eat some food. Alternatively you can shelter out of the wind until daylight then establish your position before proceeding down to safety.

Note:- It is always advisable, particularly in this situation, to have with you the items recommended in the equipment list described earlier. In the modern age of technology, a mobile telephone may be of use in this situation, reception permitting.

POST WALK

On arriving back in Horton in Ribblesdale you should return to the café to 'clock back in'. Ask for your card at the counter.

The town of Settle is only a few miles away where there is the Fishermans Rest fish and chip shop as well as a selection of public houses to cater for all tastes. There are 2 public bars in Horton.

If you have completed the 3 peaks in less than 12 hours and 'clock out/in' correctly then a few weeks later you should receive a letter to invite you to apply for membership of the 3 Peaks of Yorkshire club.

Each year on the last Sunday of April, the 3 peaks race takes place. This obviously undulating and strenuous course takes around 2hours and 30minutes for the fastest athletes to complete. The race is run under strict rules and there is a limit of 200 runners on the set route. Perhaps those walkers who like more of a challenge may apply to enter the race!

ITEMS OF INTEREST ON ROUTE

Within the village of Horton in Ribblesdale there are a number of ameneties and places of interest.

Arriving in Horton, there is a large car park (charge) with public toilets situated close by. The famous Pen-y-ghent café is just a short distance away. It is also a tourist information centre with books and walking equipment on sale.

Further along the road is Holme Farm campsite. This is frequently used by walkers and backpackers. Across the road is the local church which is dedicated to St. Oswald and is generally of Norman Style. This is worth a visit when passing.

The River Ribble meanders its way through the village going under several bridges. After leaving the river on your left you begin walking up Pen-y-ghent, there are good views back towards Horton and the quarry beyond, also of Whernside and Ingleborough.

Proceed along the route and once over Pen-y-ghent summit you can see Ribblehead Viaduct in the distance and in the valley below Hull Pot, a well known pot hole. Walking towards Whernside, Ribblehead Viaduct can be seen more clearly. Beneath the viaduct there is a monument and cairn dedicated to the building and subsequent restoration of the viaduct by British Rail and to those who built it.

Passing close to the viaduct by the railway line, you may see numerous steam train enthusiasts all armed with cameras who appear if a train is about to pass.

On the summit of Whernside there are spectacular views across to the west and Morecambe Bay as well as the mountains of the Lake District to the north, (weather permitting).

In the valley between Whernside and Ingleborough there is a natural rest stop at the Old Hill Inn. This place provides good food and a wide selection of drinks as well as camping for backpackers in a field at the side of the Inn. It is important to stress that alchohol consumed in quantity can be dangerous to the walker as it can give a false sense of security, as well as making you unsteady while walking.

On gaining the summit of Ingleborough you again have good views of Morecambe Bay and of the path to Horton the opposite way.

Overall, the scenery and open moorland views looking up to the peaks or down the valleys is spectacular and well worth the effort in doing this circular walk.

Summer Flowers to be seen on route:-

Oxeye Daisy	Heather	Daisy
Dandelion	White Clover	Tufted Vetch
Soft Rush	Thorny Purple Thistle	Harebell
Common Vetch	Willow Herb	Primrose
Meadow Thistle	Buttercup	

USEFUL INFORMATION

Campsites

- Holme Farm camp site in Horton in Ribblesdale.
  Tel 01729 860281
- The Old Hill Inn campsite in Chapel le Dale.
  Booking in advance. Tel 01524 241256
- Knight Stainforth Hall. Tel 01729 822200

B&B Selection

- The Willows, Horton in Ribblesdale, Settle,
  N. Yorks, BD24OHT Tel/Fax 01729- 860373
- Mrs E. Eaton, Husbands Barn, Stainforth, Settle,
  N. Yorks. BD24 9PB Tel 01729 822240
  http://www.husbands.force9.co.uk
- The Hikers Guest House, 3 Pen-y-ghent View,
  Horton in Ribblesdale, BD24 OHE
  Tel/Fax 01729-860300

Heights of Peaks

Pen-y-ghent	694m.	2277ft.
Whernside	736m.	2414ft.
Ingleborough	723m.	2372ft.

Walking Times

Time to complete this walk is usually between 9 - 13 hours. A typical breakdown of section times is as follows:-

Horton in Ribblesdale to Pen-y-ghent summit	1 hr 10 min.
Pen-y-ghent summit to Ribblehead	2 hr 25 min.
Ribblehead to Force Gill	45 min.
Force Gill to Whernside Summit	1 hr 00 min.
Whernside Summit to The Old Hill Inn	1 hr 15 min.
The Old Hill Inn to Ingleborough Summit	1 hr 30 min.
Ingleborough Summit to Horton in Ribblesdale	2 hr 10 min.

TOTAL   10 hr 15 min.

Add extra time for breaks on route, size of party, weather conditions and fitness of group/individuals. It is advisable to start this walk around 6-9am and plan to finish before darkness.

Grid References

Horton in Ribblesdale Car Park	G.R.808726
Pen-y-ghent Summit	G.R.839734
Ribblehead Viaduct	G.R.760794
Whernside Summit	G.R.738814
The Old Hill Inn	G.R.743776
Ingleborough Summit	G.R.741746

Grid references are given here and throughout the route description particularly to assist walkers who have G.P.S. systems to identify with places on route.

Distances to nearest main villages (by most direct route)

Pen-y-ghent summit to Horton   2.7 miles/4.4km.
Whernside summit   to Ingleton Village 7.1 miles/11.4km
Ingleborough summit to Ingleton Village 3.4 miles/5.5km.
Ingleborough summit to Horton   4.9 miles/7.9 km.

Nearest Telephones on route

Horton in Ribblesdale car park entrance.
Horton in Ribblesdale Station.
The Station Inn Pub, just up the road from Ribblehead Viaduct.
The Old Hill Inn, telephone box outside.

T.I.Cs in the 3 Peaks Area

Horton in Ribblesdale   01729 860333
Settle   01729 825192
Pateley Bridge   01423 711147
Ingleton   01524 241049

All the T.I.Cs will be pleased to offer help and advice to ensure you enjoy your visit to the Yorkshire Dales.

National Park Centres

The following National Park Centres will also be pleased to assist walkers and other visitors to the Dales with any queries.

Aysgarth Falls	01969 663424
Clapham	01524 251419
Grassington	01756 752774
Hawes	01969 667450
Malham	01729 830363
Sedberg	01539 620125

Public Houses/Refreshments

The Crown Hotel, Horton
Golden Lion Hotel, Horton
Mobile Tea Bar, Ribblehead
The Station Inn, Near Ribblehead
Philpin Snack Bar, Chapel le Dale
The Old Hill Inn, Chapel le Dale

Useful Addresses /Telephone Numbers

Long Distance Walkers Association
Brian Smith
10 Temple Park Close, Leeds LS15 0JJ
Tel: 0113 2642205
This association is set up to further the interests of those who enjoy long distance walking. Members receive a journal three times each year which includes information on all aspects of long distance walking.

Ramblers Association
2nd Floor, Camelford House,
87-90, Albert Embankment, London SE1 7TW
Local groups with regular meetings.

Yorkshire Dales National Park Authority
Tel: 01969 650456
The authority helps look after the National Park, protecting its wildlife, natural beauty and cultural heritage whilst promoting opportunities for the understanding and enjoyment of the park.

The Yorkshire Dales Society
Tel: 01943 461938
A charity that cares for the environment, cultural heritage and the people who live and work in the Yorkshire Dales.

Yorkshire Wildlife Trust
Tel: 01904 659570

Yorkshire Dales Millennium Trust
Tel: 01524 251004

The National Trust
Tel: 01904 771934

British Trust for Conservation Volunteers
Tel: 01748 811970

GLOSSARY OF WORDS

B&B - Bed and breakfast.

Bearing - A degree or number of degrees set on a compass then follow the direction of travel arrow to walk on that bearing to reach your intended destination.

Beck - Stream or Brook.

Dyke, Dike, Ditch - Words used to denote a long ridge of earth or a water channel either raised up or below normal level.

G.P.S. - Global Positioning System.

Grid Reference - Derived from the National grid reference system. This is used to pinpoint a place on a map by the use of letters and numbers, written as G.R. _ _ _ _ _ _

Gully - A narrow channel or cleft in a rockface, may have waterfalls and can be very slippery with vertical drops.

Magnetic Bearing - This is a grid bearing taken from a map and the relevant magnetic variation added to it to obtain the magnetic bearing. See the relevant maps for details of current magnetic variation.

Metalled Road - Generally known as a stone chipping road. This term evolved and became known as the roads metal or the roads surface.

Outcrop - Part of a rock formation that protrudes from the main body of rock.

Path - A narrow path of grass, mud, stone etc. suitable for walkers. Not usually more than 2m wide.

Plateau - A wide and mainly flat area of elevated land.

Summit - The highest point of a mountain or hill.

Tarn - A small landlocked mountain lake.

T.I.C. - Tourist information centre.

Track - A road (possibly rough) usually wide enough for a vehicle and often leading to a farm.

Trig Point - True name is triangulation pillar. These mark the summit of many mountains, but not every mountain has one. It is a small stone pillar with a number on it. The height of the mountain is taken from this point.